NARCOTICS: DANGEROUS PAINKILLERS

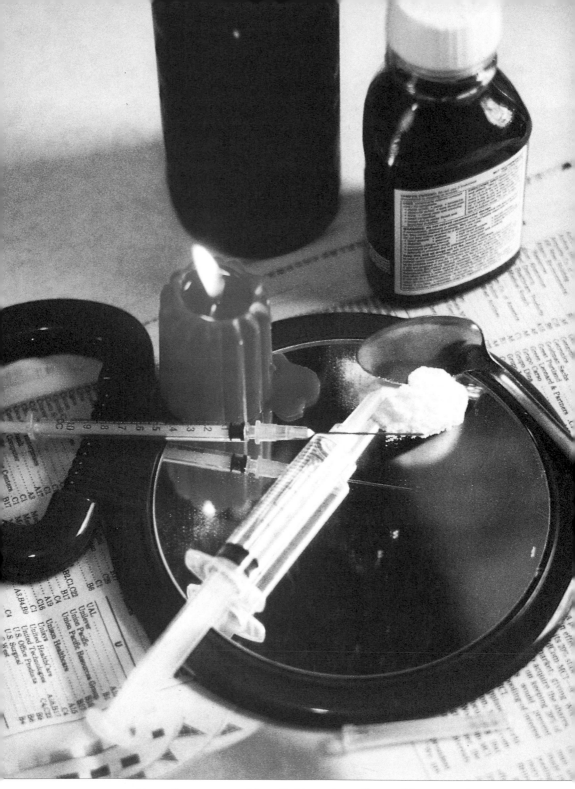

Narcotics can provide relief to pain sufferers. However, they are extremely addictive and are often abused.

THE DRUG ABUSE PREVENTION LIBRARY

NARCOTICS: DANGEROUS PAINKILLERS

George Glass

THE ROSEN PUBLISHING GROUP, INC.
NEW YORK

Published in 1998 by The Rosen Publishing Group, Inc.
29 East 21st Street, New York, NY 10010

First Edition

Library of Congress Cataloging-in-Publication Data
Glass, George, 1970-
    Narcotics: dangerous painkillers / George Glass.
        p. cm. — (The drug abuse prevention library)
    Includes bibliographical references and index.
    Summary: Describes narcotics, presents their dangers, and provides advice on how to get help when a person is addicted.
    ISBN 0-8239-2719-9
    1. Heroin habit—Juvenile literature. 2. Narcotics—Juvenile literature. [1. Narcotics. 2. Heroin. 3. Drug abuse.] I. Title. II. Series.
RC566.G56   1998
616.86'32—dc21   97-44384
                                                                   CIP
                                                                    AC

Manufactured in the United States of America

16.95

Contents

Introduction

People take drugs for many reasons. One of the most common reasons is to ease pain. Whether their pain is physical, emotional, or spiritual, many people try to feel better by using drugs. Some people use drugs safely, and others unsafely. The only time it is safe to take drugs to treat any kind of pain is when medicine is prescribed by a doctor, or bought at a drugstore and used according to the instructions on the label.

Narcotics are drugs that are known for their ability to ease pain. Many of them are natural opiates, which are made from the opium poppy—a plant that produces beautiful flowers. Others are synthetic, or human-made, drugs that provide effects similar to natural opiates.

Doctors have been prescribing narcotics for centuries to help people ease pain. But narcotics are also highly addictive and are often abused. People buy and sell them on the street, which is illegal. Taking narcotics without a doctor's prescription is extremely dangerous. Doctors know when it is appropriate to take narcotics, what the proper dosage is, and that the drugs they prescribe are pure.

When people experience pain in their bodies, they usually go to a doctor to learn how to treat the pain. But when they are hurting emotionally, some people turn to illegal substances to escape their unhappiness. This only seems to work for a very short time, and then the pain always gets worse. It is very important to experience and deal with all of your feelings, even the unpleasant ones. Using drugs to shut them out only makes your wounds take longer to heal.

Whether teens get involved with narcotics to escape their own pain, to satisfy their curiosity, or to try to have a good time, there are serious dangers involved. This book will explain those dangers, including the often fatal problems of addiction and withdrawal. You will also learn about some of the medical uses of narcotics.

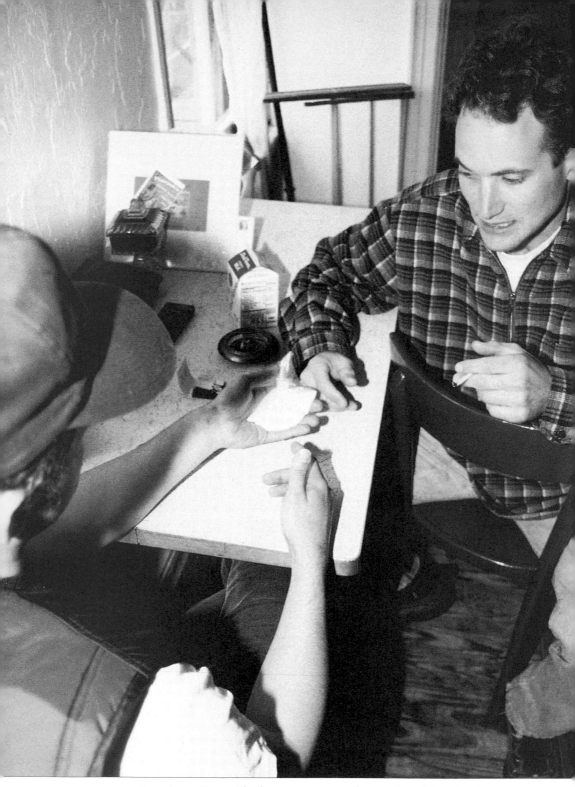

Experimenting with drugs may seem fun and exciting, but it can lead to a lifelong addiction.

CHAPTER 1

What Are Narcotics?

*A*lex is a sixteen-year-old homeless narcotic addict. He knows he is an addict, but he does not remember how he got hooked. He remembers hanging out with his best friend, Sarah. They used to experiment with different drugs. They tried marijuana, cocaine, LSD, and Ecstasy. Alex suggested heroin, but Sarah refused to try.

Alex was curious. He wanted to know what the big deal was. He was uneasy about heroin because of its reputation, but that also made him want to try it more. So he bought some from Jon, his dealer. When he showed the bag of white powder to Sarah, she called him crazy. "Alex, I'm not sure that I want to keep taking any drugs, especially heroin," she said. "I've been thinking about quitting. I want to get a

10 | job, and I can't keep fooling around with this stuff."

Alex laughed and waved the bag in front of her. "Come on, this is it! The Big H! Aren't you curious?"

Sarah sighed. "I am curious, but I don't even want to know how good it feels. It's just too dangerous."

That night, Alex tried the heroin. Jon came over to help. When Alex plunged the needle into his arm, he became dizzy and felt nauseated. He felt anything but high. "You don't usually feel it the first time," Jon said. "We'll try it again in a few days."

When Alex shot up the second time, he felt the intense high that he had heard about. It seemed like the most powerful thing he had ever felt. "Why would anyone ever want to do any other drug?" he wondered. "I could do this all the time!"

So Alex started shooting up every day. The more he did heroin, the less he cared about anything else, including his family and friends. He quit school and started stealing from his parents to support his addiction. When he couldn't get heroin, he would find morphine, Percodan, or even cough syrup with codeine, to satisfy his cravings and help calm himself down. Finally, his parents kicked him out of their house, and he had no friends left to turn to.

Narcotics include opiates, or drugs made from the opium poppy, as well as synthetic drugs created to act like opiates. They are highly addictive substances that, like depressants—such as alcohol—slow down the user's central nervous system. This means that bodily functions slow down. The main difference between narcotics and depressants is that narcotics also provide pain relief.

Other effects from narcotics may include euphoria, sleepiness, numbness, slow breathing, constipation, and nausea. Vomiting often occurs in first-time users. Most users drift between energetic and sleepy states referred to as being "on the nod."

People have chemicals in their bodies called endorphins that make them feel good and help to relieve intense pain naturally. The body releases these chemicals when we laugh, exercise, or feel pain. Narcotics imitate these natural chemicals to relieve pain and to create unnatural highs and feelings of well-being. But people build up a tolerance to narcotics, which means that users need to take more of the drug each time to feel the same high. Eventually users will not get a high anymore. Instead they will have to take the drug only to help relieve withdrawal symptoms—the

12 | painful physical and psychological reactions that an addict experiences when he or she stops taking a drug.

Here are some of the most common narcotics and how they are often used or abused:

Opium

Opium is a gum-like substance collected from opium poppies using a special knife. It is converted to a harder substance, which can be smoked. Smoking opium is highly addictive, illegal, and relatively uncommon in the United States today.

Opium can be prepared in other ways and used as medicine. For example, some doctors prescribe granulated opium and camphorated tincture of opium (a liquid) for diarrhea. Opium is also used to make other illegal drugs, such as heroin, which is described later.

Morphine and "The God of Dreams"

The natural opiate morphine is said to be named for the god of dreams, Morpheus. This is probably because of morphine's powerful ability to relieve pain and induce sleep.

Morphine is the main substance in opium that produces the opiate effects. It is considered the most effective pain

Narcotics may cause a user to feel nauseated, sleepy, and numb.

14 reliever. Manufactured, both legally and illegally, from the opium poppy in factories worldwide, it generally appears in white crystal or powder form. Usually, morphine is prescribed by doctors to patients with chronic pain. It has been found to relieve pain in nearly 95 percent of cancer cases. However, it is often abused because of the high it can produce.

This high and the drug's addictiveness have made doctors hesitant to prescribe morphine in the past. But today, morphine pills that are not addictive and do not produce a high have been developed. They help many people who suffer from ailments like back pain or cancer.

The "Big H": Heroin

Heroin, also known as "Big H," "Brown," "Horse," "Junk," "Scag," or "Smack," is the most well-known and most abused narcotic. It is a natural opiate, created from morphine. In the past, heroin was thought to be a cure for morphine addiction. However, it was later discovered to be two to three times more powerful than morphine. Today, heroin is not used for any medical purposes.

According to Missouri's Division of Alcohol and Drug Abuse, heroin accounts for 90 percent of the opiate abuse in the

United States, and abuse continues to rise. In 1995 the National Household Survey on Drug Abuse found that 1.4 million people have used heroin, twice as many people as in 1994. Not coincidentally, there has also been a steady increase in heroin-related emergency hospital visits, from 38,100 in 1988 to 75,912 in 1995.

Usually appearing as a white or brown powder, heroin may be "cut" by drug dealers with other substances, such as sugar—which leads to varying purity levels. Dealers may also cut heroin with poisons that may be fatal.

Heroin can be swallowed, smoked, or snorted, but the most intense high is obtained when it is injected under the skin (skin popping) or into a vein (mainlining). "Chasing the dragon" describes the inhaling of the fumes that are released when heroin is heated.

After a user takes a hit, he or she feels an intense "rush" for a few minutes. This rush becomes a less intense high that usually lasts about four or five hours. During this time a user may feel warm and cozy. Then comes withdrawal.

It surprises many heroin users that after they have used the drug for a while, they no longer get high. Their bodies develop a

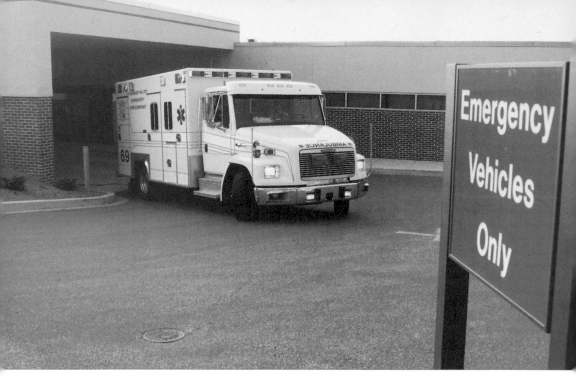

Heroin-related emergency hospital visits have been steadily increasing since the late-1980s.

tolerance to the drug. But, at this point, the user can't stop using heroin without experiencing painful withdrawal symptoms. Many users die from heroin overdoses as they use more of the drug trying to get the high. Because a heroin user's body is so dependent on the drug, withdrawal should not be attempted without professional help.

China White

China White is a synthetic narcotic, created to act like heroin. It is considered a designer drug, because it is made in illegal laboratories by unskilled people.

Drug dealers may buy China White and pass it off as heroin, because it is cheaper.

Many people may not know they are taking China White, which is more dangerous than heroin because it is more powerful. This means that less China White is needed to get the same high as heroin, making it easier to overdose.

China White is a white powder, similar to heroin. It can be injected, smoked, or snorted and is extremely dangerous and addictive. In Philadelphia, Pennsylvania, twenty-one people overdosed on it during two months in 1992. China White can cause severe constipation, heart failure, uncontrollable shaking, slow breathing, paralysis, and death by overdose.

Methadone
Methadone is a synthetic narcotic that may be used for medical purposes. It is used primarily by narcotic addicts to combat withdrawal symptoms. Methadone is legal when administered by doctors for this purpose. It is a white powder which can be dissolved in liquid, and is generally taken orally.

While methadone can be used to help recovering addicts, it has the potential for abuse. Therefore, it is only given to narcotic addicts under the guidance of a trained professional. When administered properly, methadone does not produce a high in an

18 | addict. It only needs to be administered once a day during treatment, because the effects of methadone can last as long as twenty-four hours.

Narcotics Not Commonly Abused

The following drugs are more commonly used for medical purposes than abused by addicts. However, many addicts get these drugs from medical sources—by forging prescriptions or by stealing the drugs—to replace their drug of choice, or to avoid withdrawal. Some of these drugs, even if legally prescribed, can cause narcotic addiction. This is why their use needs to be closely monitored by a doctor.

Codeine the "Poppyhead"

Codeine (which comes from the Greek word *kodeia* meaning "poppyhead") is a natural opiate. It appears in both white powder and crystal form, and is used in prescription cough syrups or pain relievers. It is similar to morphine, but much less potent. Codeine is not abused very often. Today, more controls exist for prescribing codeine, so there is less potential for abuse.

Demerol

A synthetic narcotic, Demerol is used medically and is sometimes abused, affecting the

Even when narcotics are legally prescribed by a doctor, the potential for addiction is high.

user like morphine. It comes in the form of pills or in a banana-flavored syrup.

Dilaudid

Dilaudid is a natural opiate that is about two to eight times more potent than morphine. Developed in Germany in the early 1920s, some doctors prescribed it instead of morphine because they believed it was nonaddictive. In 1935 Dilaudid was proven to be extremely addictive. Today, it is still used for medical purposes and is sought out by narcotic addicts through medical sources.

Hydrocodone

A natural opiate, hydrocodone is a commonly prescribed pain reliever that is taken in syrup, tablet, or capsule form.

20 |

Metopon

Metopon is a natural opiate that is used medically to relieve pain. It is preferable to morphine in certain cases, because it numbs pain without severely slowing mental activity.

Percocet and Percodan

Percocet and Percodan are prescription pain relievers containing a drug called oxycodone. Oxycodone is a natural opiate more powerful and addictive than codeine. It usually appears as a white powder.

Phenazocine

A synthetic narcotic, Phenazocine is very powerful, but it is less addictive than many other narcotic drugs.

Both science and nature provide us with substances to help us deal with physical pain. There is nothing wrong with taking advantage of these benefits when in need. The key is using good judgment and moderation. There are professionals who know how to use the gifts of nature and science safely. Taking drugs without their guidance is an unnecessary and potentially fatal risk.

CHAPTER 2

The History of Narcotics

People have known about the effects of the opium poppy since prehistoric times. Around 4000 BC, this flower was referred to by Sumerian peoples in Asia Minor as *hul gil*, which means "plant of joy." Evidence of opium use has also been found in Egyptian documents from 1500 BC.

Opium use spread from Egypt to Greece, then to India and China. Smoking opium became popular in China, and the Chinese government attempted to control how much entered its country.

Since Britain made a lot of money in the opium trade, it did not want China's laws to regulate the flow of opium. This conflict resulted in the Opium War, which lasted from 1839 to 1842. The British won this

Opium is found in these plants called opium poppies.

war, which led to the legalization of the opium trade in China. Soon opium smoking spread to the United States.

Laudanum (opium and alcohol) was developed in the early 1500s. It was used in Europe for coughs, dysentery, and general pain relief. In 1803 a German pharmacist named F. W. Sertürner discovered the active substance in opium, and named it morphine. It became a common painkiller and many people became addicted to it quickly. About 400,000 soldiers became morphine addicts during the Civil War. They had used it to ease the pain of their injuries.

Opium was legal and common in the nineteenth century in America. Opiate syrups and powders were sold over the counter at drugstores, and were recommended by doctors for everything from children's teething pain to diarrhea.

Many people also took opium to get high even though it was not respectable to use opium for pleasure. Most opium users at this time were women between the ages of twenty-five and fifty-five.

Heroin was first made from morphine in 1874 by English researcher C. R. Wright. People thought it would combat morphine addiction. Instead, it proved to be even

24 more addictive. In fact, it is so addictive that it is not used for medical purposes.

Heroin experienced a surge in popularity among youth in the 1990s. It has become less expensive and purer since the 1980s. Purity levels rose from an average of 2 to 8 percent in the 1980s to more than 50 percent in the mid-1990s. Greater purity means that heroin can be smoked or snorted, attracting users who are wary of shooting up. The danger of the shift in purity levels is that you don't have any way of knowing how much stronger the drug is, which can result in an overdose.

Many popular celebrities have died of heroin overdoses. Jonathan Melvoin of the band Smashing Pumpkins died in 1996 of an overdose. He was thirty-four. Shannon Hoon, a twenty-three-year-old singer in the band Blind Melon, died of an overdose in 1995. Other deaths linked to heroin include photographer David Sorrenti, vocalist Brad Nowell of Sublime, Hole's Kristin Pfaff, and actor River Phoenix. Just think of all the music and art the world could have enjoyed if so many talented people's lives had not been cut short.

"Heroin Chic" in the 1990s

"Heroin chic" is a phrase used to describe

the glamorization of heroin use in fashion, music, movies, and other areas of popular culture. Fashion designer Calvin Klein has been criticized for using models who resemble drug addicts in his ad campaigns. Fashion spreads for certain magazines have featured models who resemble addicts, in settings and situations that strongly suggest drug use. Movies like *Trainspotting* and *Pulp Fiction*, which also show the dangers of drug use, have been criticized for making heroin seem exciting.

In 1997 President Bill Clinton spoke against heroin chic in the media. Producers of these images insist they merely reflect our troubled times, and that blaming them for the problem does nothing to address the root of the problem. Most people believe that the media both reflect and influence our society, including our attitudes about problems such as heroin abuse. Unfortunately, this is not a simple issue that has a simple solution.

Laws and Legislation

Smoking opium was banned in San Francisco and several other Californian cities in 1875. In 1887 a law was passed by Congress prohibiting the importation of a special kind of opium used mainly for smoking.

26   In 1906 Congress passed the Pure Food and Drug Act. Products containing opium had to label how much opium was included. These medicines had to meet certain government standards of purity.

The next major law to regulate narcotics—and cocaine, which is not a narcotic—was the Harrison Narcotic Act of 1914. It required narcotics sellers to be licensed, and it restricted the amount of opium used in over-the-counter medicines.

A few years later, government committees discovered an increase in narcotic addiction and a growth of the underground drug economy. Organized illegal smuggling of narcotics across American borders had also increased. Congress decided to create more strict drug laws and restrictions. Many people have since questioned their effectiveness.

In 1970 Congress introduced the Controlled Substances Act, which classifies and regulates the use of drugs that have a potential for abuse, including narcotics, into five categories. The most restrictive category, Schedule I, includes drugs that are highly addictive and have no medical use in the United States. Heroin falls into this category. Schedule II drugs are also highly addictive but do have medical use in

The talented young actor River Phoenix cut his life short when he died from an overdose of heroin and cocaine.

28 the United States, such as morphine and methadone. Schedule III, IV, and V drugs are not as addictive as the drugs in the first two schedules, but are still dangerous. Narcotics in these lower categories may include opium and codeine.

Currently all drug regulations and law enforcement are handled by the Drug Enforcement Administration (DEA), which was established on July 1, 1973.

The International Drug Problem

Many countries were responding to problems of worldwide drug abuse in the early 1900s. China limited its opium production in 1907, and India agreed to stop exporting opium to China. In 1909, thirteen nations came together in Shanghai for the first International Opium Commission. Laws and treaties were drawn up to control the opium trade.

After World War II, primary responsibility for creating and enforcing these sorts of laws was passed on to the World Health Organization. This international agency still plays an extremely important role in worldwide drug control.

The Golden Triangle and Golden Crescent

The "Golden Triangle" was the world's

largest producer of opium during the 1960s and 1970s. It is a name given to an area in Southeast Asia that includes Thailand, Northern Laos, and Eastern Burma. In the late 1970s, opium production in this area declined due to increased law enforcement and poor crops.

Soon the "Golden Crescent" replaced the Golden Triangle as the leader in opium production. The Golden Crescent, which is in Southwest Asia, includes Afghanistan, Iran, and Pakistan.

In 1996, according to the DEA, Southeast Asia was once again the leader in opium production. However, since South America (mainly Colombia) converts almost all of its opium to heroin, it—along with Southeast Asia—is a major source of the heroin in the United States.

Using History to Make Decisions About Narcotics

It is important to learn about the past to make decisions about your future. You can learn from the sad, untimely deaths of people like River Phoenix and Jonathan Melvoin; such tragedies need not occur in our own lives.

CHAPTER 3

Abuse, Addiction, and Withdrawal

*M*r. Johnson had a terrible cough for about a week. It had been keeping him awake every night, and he finally decided to see his doctor. She told him to get plenty of rest, and prescribed a cough syrup with codeine for him to take three times each day. He followed the instructions on the label and took one teaspoonful before bed that night. The codeine quieted his cough and helped him to relax and sleep.

After he went to sleep, his sons, Felix and Joe, noticed the medicine in the kitchen. Felix, who was fifteen, said, "Hey, this has codeine. I heard that it can get you really messed up." "Really?" asked Joe, who was fourteen. "Yeah, better than beer," said Felix. He took a large swig from the bottle, about three times the adult dosage. He handed the bottle to Joe, who immediately began *gulping the syrup. "Hey, slow down. Dad will notice this much gone!" said Felix.*

He replaced what they had taken with water, and shook the bottle. Pretty soon the brothers felt warm and tingly. "Hey, this is really cool!" said Joe. Soon, however, the warmth and tingling turned to sweating and nausea. "I'm gonna be sick!" said Felix, running to the bathroom.

They both felt so sick they had to wake their father and tell him what they had done. He rushed them to the hospital and they had to have their stomachs pumped.

Drug abuse can also sometimes be called drug misuse. According to the Food and Drug Administration, drug abuse means taking a drug for a different reason than was intended, in a way that could do harm to the user. In this example, Mr. Johnson was using codeine for its intended purpose; to help him stop coughing and to get better. This was the doctor's intention when she prescribed the medication.

But his sons, Felix and Joe, misused the medication. They abused codeine by using it for the purpose of "getting messed up." This was not why it was prescribed, and the boys were putting themselves in great danger.

32 Drug addiction and abuse often occur at the same time. In general, addiction refers to dependence upon the effects of a drug. Physical dependence refers to the body's need to keep taking a certain drug. Without the drug, the body cannot function properly and the addict experiences withdrawal—symptoms ranging from discomfort to great pain. Withdrawal from a drug can be very harmful if not done under medical supervision.

Psychological dependence means addiction that occurs in the user's mind. Many people believe if a drug is not physically addictive, they cannot become dependent upon it. But psychological addiction is very powerful and can last much longer than physical dependence. No matter how strong or healthy someone is mentally, it is very easy to become dependent on an artificial high.

Heroin, for example, is both physically and psychologically addictive. Users experience painful physical withdrawal when they try to stop. But they also become psychologically addicted. Addicts stop caring about important areas of life, such as family, friends, school, their careers, and their interests. All they care about is getting high. They feel they cannot survive in the world without heroin. The psychological

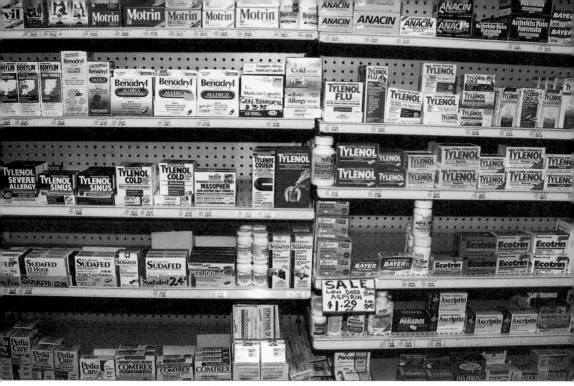

Many over-the-counter drugs offer a safe option for pain relief.

effects of heroin and other narcotics can be devastating.

Just about anyone who becomes addicted to drugs believes at first that it could not happen to them. According to the National Parents' Resource Institute for Drug Addiction (PRIDE), nearly one in five twelfth graders in 1996 used an illegal drug every week or more, and almost one in ten used daily. Most of these young people probably did not believe they were addicted.

Since most people do not know if they have an addictive personality or not, it is a good idea to avoid experimenting with illegal narcotics. Sometimes just one try is all it takes to become addicted.

34

Narcotics and AIDS

There are several reasons why abusing narcotics, or any drugs, can put you at great risk for contracting HIV, the virus that causes AIDS. Drugs lower inhibitions. This is one of the reasons some people enjoy taking them. Drugs can make people feel more free to do things they would not ordinarily do, without worrying about the consequences of their actions.

Sometimes those actions can, unfortunately, have painful or fatal consequences. Someone may get high and have unprotected sex with one or more partners. This loss of control can lead to any number of sexually transmitted diseases, including AIDS.

There is also the risk of contracting HIV by sharing needles. This is mainly a concern among heroin users, although many drugs can be injected. Injecting a needle that has been used by other people without cleaning it first with bleach can transmit many diseases or infections the previous user might have had, including HIV. Intravenous drug users are the second largest high-risk group for AIDS.

Narcotics and Pregnancy

It is dangerous for pregnant women to take any drugs not prescribed by a doctor, and

Taking narcotics during pregnancy is extremely dangerous for both the mother and the baby.

36 this includes narcotics. It is estimated that about half of the pregnant women who are dependent on opiates such as heroin suffer from anemia, heart disease, diabetes, pneumonia, or hepatitis during pregnancy and childbirth. They are also more likely than other women to have spontaneous abortions, premature births, and stillbirths. The babies that are born under these conditions, if they survive, can suffer withdrawal symptoms for several months. Abusing drugs while pregnant puts both mother and child at great risk.

It is possible, however, for women receiving methadone treatment to deliver healthy babies. The infants may experience some mild, treatable withdrawal symptoms, but these symptoms are minor compared to the complications that can arise from heroin use during pregnancy.

Since narcotics can appear in breast milk and could harm a baby, it is important for women who are breastfeeding to not take any narcotics—including those that are prescribed, unless directed by a doctor.

Withdrawal from Narcotics

We have discussed the extremely addictive nature of narcotics. So what happens when an addict tries to stop? When a user who is

physically addicted to a drug suddenly
stops using it, the body goes through withdrawal. For narcotic addicts, withdrawal is
extremely severe.

Withdrawal symptoms are not the same
for all addicts. The stronger and purer the
drug, and the more frequently it is used, the
more intense and painful withdrawal will be.
It is important that anyone quitting narcotics seek professional help.

At first, symptoms of withdrawal from
narcotics may appear to the user to be like
cold or flu symptoms. They can include
aches, chills, sweating, a runny nose,
nausea, and anxiety. Soon these feelings
become extremely intense, and other
symptoms appear. The user may twitch
and convulse uncontrollably. Diarrhea is
common, partly as a result of constipation
throughout the duration of the narcotic
addiction. The user's heart may race, and
sleep could become nearly impossible.

Withdrawal reaches its most intensely
painful point about twenty-four to forty-
eight hours after use of the drug has
stopped. Many addicts do not make it past
the excruciating peak, and soon go in
search of more narcotics to stop the pain.
This is one reason methadone treatment is
often successful for heroin addiction. It can

38 ease the severity of this stage of withdrawal. Although methadone is also a narcotic, it has a much more gradual and less painful withdrawal period.

Heroin withdrawal generally lasts about one week, although some symptoms can continue for up to six months. And though the physical addiction ends, psychological dependence may continue indefinitely. Symptoms of psychological dependence include anxiety, depression, and strong drug cravings.

Withdrawal from narcotics generally creates feelings that are the opposite of what users were looking for when they began taking drugs. The euphoria created by opium, heroin, or morphine is replaced with severe pain and anxiety. Many drugs ultimately have this effect. They often lead users in a circle, promising paradise but leading to torment. An intense drug high is almost always followed by an intense low.

CHAPTER 4

How Does Drug Addiction Begin?

*D*awn liked marijuana. "I drink and I get high, it's no big deal," Dawn explained when her mother found a stash under Dawn's bed. "It's not like I'm shooting heroin or something." Her mother was unhappy about her daughter's drug use, but she figured most kids did the same thing. And the drugs Dawn used seemed pretty harmless, so she didn't push it.

Dawn was an unhappy teen. She'd had a rough childhood. She had never really dealt with many of the painful things that had happened to her. She insisted that she didn't use drugs to numb her feelings. Actually, she was blind to the true reasons for her drug use.

One night, Dawn's friend Samantha took her to a party where she hardly knew anyone. The people there were all much older than her, and they seemed very cool. Everyone was drinking,

A person can become addicted to a narcotic even after the first time he or she takes it.

so Dawn had a couple of beers. That helped her to loosen up and not feel so awkward.

She ended up sitting on the floor with six other people. They were all passing a joint around and giggling hysterically about something. Not wanting to be left out, Dawn took a few hits from the joint. She was just starting to feel part of the conversation, when suddenly Samantha pulled her away by the arm.

"I found out what's going on here tonight," said Samantha. "Someone is bringing serious drugs. I heard they're even doing heroin."

Dawn was kind of thrown by this, but she was also pretty high. "That doesn't mean we can't hang out here," she protested. "Everyone seems really cool." Samantha didn't want to stay, so she left.

Dawn smoked more marijuana and began talking and laughing with the others. She felt like she was bonding with them. Then one of them pulled out some drug works. "I have a surprise tonight," he said. "If you try this, you'll never want any other drug."

Dawn watched the young man tie a piece of plastic around his arm and plunge a needle into his vein. Dawn had promised herself she would stay away from serious drugs. But this seemed fun, and it couldn't hurt to try once. "I'll try some," she said.

She looked at the needle. It glistened, and seemed almost pretty, in a strange way. Maybe heroin isn't so bad, she thought. "Will you help me?" she asked the boy.

He smiled. "Of course," he said. He tied the plastic around her arm and injected the needle. She felt dizzy, then she felt sick, then she felt a warm sensation flood her stomach.

"This is interesting," she said, leaning against a wall. For a moment, she felt like she was being swept down a warm river very quickly. Then everything went black.

She woke up in a hospital room. Her mother sat next to her. "Oh no," Dawn thought. "Think fast." Her mother took her hand. "Hi, mom," she said, shaking. "I . . . I don't know what happened. Someone must have slipped something into my drink."

42

Her mother stared down at her. "That's what I thought at first," said her mother. "But the doctor told me you shot heroin into your arm! Why would you do that?"

Dawn stared at the ceiling. "I don't know," she said. "I guess I thought it might be fun."

As soon as she got out of the hospital, she went straight for her stash of marijuana. She hoped it might calm her down. Why didn't she stop when she was at the party? She stared at the joint in her hand and really began to wonder.

This story shows one way that drug addiction can begin. Nobody plans to become addicted to drugs. Often misinformation and some common false beliefs leave people vulnerable to drug addiction.

The following are some of the myths about using drugs:

Alcohol and marijuana are safe drugs.

Alcohol and marijuana have been called "gateway drugs." This means that using alcohol or marijuana may lead to using harder drugs as the user searches for a more intense high. Many people who claim they will never touch "serious" drugs will still drink and smoke pot.

Alcohol and marijuana can impair both your physical and mental health. About 11

million people in the United States are alco- | *43*
holics, and between 16 and 20 million Amer-
icans are frequent marijuana users. Taking
alcohol or marijuana can lead to unclear
thinking and poor judgment, which could
lead to the use of other substances.

I can't get addicted the first time.

Many people also hold the false belief that
someone can't get pregnant the first time
she has sex. The truth is, addiction can
begin with the first sip, puff, or hit. It can
cause physical and/or psychological dependence.

You never know how your mind and
body will react to a substance. That is why
it makes more sense to avoid the substance altogether. You might be able to try
it once and then stop. Or you might like
it so much you'll want to do it again and
again.

If I smoke or snort heroin, it's safe because I'm not injecting it.

In 1993 there were 6,000 hospital emergency room visits related to snorting
heroin. You can become addicted to heroin
whether you smoke, snort, or inject it.
Using heroin is dangerous no matter how
you put it into your body.

44

If the drug isn't physically addictive, it is safe to use.

Many people will only try drugs that are not physically addictive. They greatly underestimate the power of psychological addiction. No matter how strong you feel mentally, you could still succumb to psychological addiction. Becoming dependent on a drug does not mean you are stupid or weak. It can happen to very bright, secure people, and the only definite way to prevent it is to avoid drugs.

I just take drugs for fun, and I could stop at any time.

More than a quarter of American twelfth graders surveyed by PRIDE admitted to using alcohol once a week. Nearly one in twenty high school students in 1995 used marijuana every day. Many people take these and other drugs to "party," but the scary thing about drug addiction is that you don't see it coming. Many people who say that they could stop taking drugs any time they want have never actually tried to stop.

An addiction warps a person's perspective on his or her own life. An addict may be blind to the fact that he or she has a drug problem. People who are dependent upon a substance will not only lie to other people,

but to themselves as well, to get the high
they crave. They may justify stealing money
from a friend by telling themselves they'll
give it back one day. Or they may tell themselves that they'll stop using when they get
a job. An addict is his or her own worst
enemy. What seems like a fun pastime could
actually be a deadly addiction in disguise.

I need drugs to be able to communicate with others.

Because a group of people using the same
drug can share a mutual state of mind,
which creates a common ground to meet
upon, drugs are most often used socially.
All human beings crave connections with
others, which can be difficult to form.
Sometimes drugs seem to make it easier.

But relying on drugs to help you relate
and share with people is extremely dangerous, and can easily lead to serious addiction.
Talking to people and socializing can be difficult, especially if you are uncomfortable in
groups. However, with a little practice,
anyone can develop social skills.

Drugs are hip and glamorous.

Certain drugs go in and out of style. LSD
may be popular among young people one
day, then inhalants could be popular the

Some people take drugs hoping to enhance their creativity, but eventually the search for drugs leaves no room for anything else.

next. It is not fun to follow fashion when
it means risking your life to be in style.

Watching our favorite musicians, ac-
tors, and artists overdose on drugs and
die young is terrifying and sad. Their
tragic deaths should serve as a reminder
of how destructive drug abuse can be.
Many of our idols, like singer and gui-
tarist Jimi Hendrix and singer Elvis
Presley, were talented people whose lives
just spun out of control. The world lost
them and their talent to drugs.

Drugs make you creative.

There is no drug on earth that can make a
person more creative. The only way to
enhance true creativity is through mental exercise and practice, not by taking drugs. If you
are truly interested in becoming more creative,
you can find many books to help you at the
library, or ask a teacher at school for ideas.

Signs to Watch For

It can be difficult to tell if you have a
problem with alcohol or drugs. Usually,
the addict is the last to figure it out. The
following are certain things to watch for
that can serve as signs of drug addiction.

Nagging of others.
If your friends or family members start

Taking drugs when you are alone is a sign that you may be addicted.

hounding you about drinking or drugging too much, don't brush them off. Sometimes others can see you better than you can see yourself, especially when you are out of control or in danger. Pay attention to the people who care about you, and take their advice seriously.

Blackouts.
When people cannot remember what they did when they were drinking or using drugs, that is a blackout. It is one of the main warning signs of a drug or alcohol problem. A blackout indicates a serious and dangerous loss of control.

Drinking or drugging alone.
Make no mistake, if people only use

drugs socially, it does not mean they are | *49*
immune to addiction. But using alone is a
definite sign that you may be addicted and
that something very deep is probably moti-
vating the drug use.

Lying.

Do you tell people you are sober when you
are high? Do you say you've had one beer
after downing half a bottle of whiskey?
Chances are you have a problem, and you
are lying in order to hide it.

Planning and fantasizing.

Do you think about what it feels like to take
drugs when you are sober? Do you anx-
iously plan your next drink or hit? Does it
seem like a "casual, recreational" drug user
would do this?

Dipping grades and/or poor job per-
formance.

Most drug users reach a point where they
don't care about anything other than
getting high. When a drug or alcohol user
stops making an effort in school or at work,
it is a definite sign that he or she has lost
control over his or her own life.

Getting sick frequently.

"Party 'til you puke," is a popular American
expression, but it is a bad sign if you are

An addict may find herself fighting more often with loved ones or losing contact with close friends.

actually doing it. Even worse is when you get sick, then immediately continue to drink or drug.

Guilt.

Addicts often feel remorseful and guilty the morning after, especially if they said or did something they regret.

Relationship problems.

Not just with your boyfriend or girlfriend, but with any or all of your friends and family. Beware when your connections with non-drug users start to slip away, or fighting increases.

Using drugs to cope or forget.

Have you ever had a drink so that you could deal with a stressful day or event? Maybe a hit of cocaine to break the ice at a party? Or how about shooting up in order to forget about your troubles for the night? This could be a warning sign of addiction.

These are warning signs you should look for in yourself and in others. If you or someone you know is experiencing any of these symptoms, it is never too late to seek help. Just do not be afraid to take the first step. Living life as a drug addict is much more terrifying than giving up drugs.

CHAPTER 5

How to Get Help

Avoiding drugs is the best way to prevent a drug problem. But not everybody avoids drugs. If you find yourself in trouble with drugs, you may feel down on yourself for getting into such a situation. Do not beat yourself up for it. It will only make things worse. Everybody makes mistakes, and it's never too late to correct them and get your life back on track again.

Realizing and admitting you have a problem is the first step to getting better. This can be difficult, because denying your real feelings is a major part of addiction. If you think that you might have a problem, find someone to talk to about it. It doesn't have to be a counselor, although that would be great. Just talk to anyone you

A first step toward recovery is admitting to someone you trust that you have a drug problem.

trust. Talking can help you sort out your feelings and figure out what to do next.

From here you have several options. It is a good idea to seek help from a trained professional. Your brother or history teacher might be great listeners, but they probably don't know what needs to be done to help you get off drugs. But there are many people who do.

Narcotics Anonymous

Narcotics Anonymous (NA) is an organization for anyone who has, or has ever had, a problem with drugs. They hold meetings, which anyone can attend, where people in recovery can safely and openly discuss their feelings. You can find information on how

54 | to contact NA at the back of this book ("Where to Go for Help"). You can also look in your local telephone book for the number of NA in your area. If you call NA in your area, they can give you a schedule of meetings and help you to figure out a plan for getting and staying clean.

Going to an NA meeting can seem a bit intimidating the first time. You probably do not know what to expect. The only requirement is that you must want to stop using drugs. It might be easier if you bring a trusted friend or family member along to the first meeting.

Many recovering addicts say they never would have gotten clean if they had not gone to an NA meeting. All you will find there are more people like you, fighting the same problems you are. It feels good to share and express your feelings with people who understand. If you are not comfortable talking about your addiction, nobody will make you say anything if you don't want to. Nobody will rush you to do anything before you are ready.

There are also other organizations that can help. Check listings in the Yellow Pages of your telephone book under Addiction, Crisis Intervention Counseling, and Drugs. You should be able to find hot lines, for when

you need to talk to someone immediately, as |
well as treatment centers that have programs
to help people with drug problems.

Methadone Treatment

Methadone treatment does not cure narcotic addiction. The idea behind this treatment is to help narcotics users reduce their withdrawal symptoms and cravings while in rehabilitation for their addiction. By giving the narcotics user a dose that is only large enough to reduce the withdrawal symptoms, it is hoped that the user is thus able to lead a productive life and start on the road to recovery while in a methadone treatment program.

There is some ongoing debate over how effective it is to use methadone in treating narcotic addiction. Some people say the treatment simply substitutes one drug addiction for another. Others insist that if the choice for addicts is between using narcotics bought on the street—which has many unknown factors—or taking methadone at a clinic while in a rehabilitation program, methadone is the safer option.

Acceptance into a methadone treatment program is based on a number of factors. For example, you must be addicted to illegal opiates for at least one year, show

Methadone treatment is not a cure for narcotic addiction, but it can help addicts regain control of their lives as they recover.

withdrawal symptoms, and have found other detoxification programs have not worked for you. If you are interested in entering a methadone treatment program, see your doctor or contact the methadone clinic nearest you.

If Someone You Know Has a Drug Problem

If your friend, brother, sister, or any other relative has a problem with drugs, it affects you. There are things you can do to help the addict, as well as to help yourself deal with the situation.

It can be extremely difficult to help people with drug problems. It puts you in a difficult position. Drug addicts may not

realize they have problems, and they probably will not be receptive to help. They can
be cruel and shut you out.

You might think you are helping them
by lying for them or lending them money
when they have spent theirs on drugs. This
can only make matters worse. You need to
get support from a professional to help you
figure out what to do. You can call any of
the numbers at the back of this book and
tell them what is going on. They should be
able to help you find a solution.

There are also organizations that can help
you cope with being a friend or relative of an
addict. Do not let his or her drug problem
consume you, and never blame yourself for
his or her behavior. Check the back of this
book for the phone number of Nar-Anon, an
organization for friends and family of
addicts. They can tell you if there is a Narateen group in your area or how to start one
if one does not exist. Narateen is for twelve
to twenty-year-olds who want to meet about
a friend's or family member's addiction.

Recovery can be a painful process, and you
will have to learn to manage your problems
in healthier ways. But won't it feel good to
have control over your life again, and not
have it in the hands of a chemical?

Glossary

drug abuse Taking a drug for a different reason than was intended.

drug addiction Physical or psychological dependence upon the effects of a drug.

forge To sign something falsely.

Golden Crescent Current leader in opium production; includes Afghanistan, Iran, and Pakistan.

Golden Triangle The world's largest producer of opium during the 1960s and 1970s; includes Thailand, Northern Laos, and Eastern Burma.

Harrison Narcotic Act A 1914 law that regulated the sale of narcotics.

narcotics Opiates, or human-made drugs that act like opiates; they slow down the user's central nervous system and provide pain relief.

Narcotics Anonymous (NA) An organization that helps drug addicts quit and stay off drugs.

opiates Drugs made from the opium poppy.

opium A gum-like substance in opium poppies; a very powerful narcotic.

opium poppy A plant from which some
   narcotics are made. It has a natural
   ability to numb pain.
Pure Food and Drug Act A 1906 law
   that regulated contents of products containing opium.
synthetic Human-made.
withdrawal A painful syndrome that
   affects a drug addict's mind and body
   when he or she stops using drugs.
World Health Organization International
   agency responsible for worldwide drug
   control.

Where to Go for Help

Hot Lines
(800) 67-PRIDE
(800) 9-FRIEND
(800) 662-HELP
Youth Crisis Hot Line
(800) 448-4663

Web Sites
Drug Enforcement Administration
http://www.usdoj.gov/dea

Organizations
American Council for Drug Education
204 Monroe Street
Rockville, MD 20852
(301) 294-0600

Nar-Anon Family Group Headquarters, Inc.
P.O. Box 2562
Palos Verdes Peninsula, CA 90274
(310) 547-5800

Narcotics Anonymous (NA)
World Service Office
19737 Nordhoff Place
Chatsworth, CA 91311
(818) 773-9999
e-mail: wso@aol.com

National Abuse Center
5530 Wisconsin Avenue, NW
Washington, DC 20015
(800)333-2294

National Clearinghouse for Alcohol and
  Drug Information
P.O. Box 2345
Rockville, MD 20847-2345
(301) 468-2600
(800) 729-6686
Web site: http://www.health.org
e-mail: info@prevline.health.org

In Canada:

Narcotics Anonymous
P.O. Box 7500
Station A
Toronto, ON M5W 1P9
(416)691-9519

For Further Reading

Allinson, Russel R. *Drug Abuse: Why It Happens and How to Prevent It.* Lower Burrell, PA: Valley Publishing, 1984.

Clayton, Lawrence, Ph.D. *Designer Drugs.* Rev. Ed. New York: Rosen Publishing Group, 1998.

Courtwright, David T. *Dark Paradise: Opiate Addiction in America Before 1940.* Cambridge, MA: Harvard University Press, 1982.

DeStefano, Susan. *Focus on Opiates: A Drug-Alert Book.* Frederick, MD: Twenty-First Century Books, 1991.

Hurwitz, Sue, and Schniderman, Nancy. *Drugs and Your Friends.* Rev. Ed. New York: Rosen Publishing Group, 1995.

Jaffe, Jerome H., ed. *Encyclopedia of Drugs and Alcohol.* New York: Macmillan Library Reference USA, 1995.

Simpson, Carolyn. *Methadone.* New York: Rosen Publishing Group, 1997.

Smith, Sandra Lee. *Heroin.* Rev. Ed. New York: Rosen Publishing Group, 1995.

Woods, Geraldine. *Heroin.* Hillside, NJ: Enslow Publishers, 1994.

Index

64

About the Author

George Glass is a freelance writer living in New York City. He is also the author of *Drugs and Fitting In*.

Photo Credits

Photo on p. 22 by Richard Pharaoh/AP/Wide World; p. 27 by AP/Wide World; p. 33 by Ira Fox; All other photos and cover by Ethan Zindler